HER FROZEN THOUGHTS

SHE IS A POET IN HER FANTASY WORLD

RAIYAAN KAUSAR

"*At the end of every dark room, there exists light and all it requires to find is a tad of patience.*"

This book is dedicated to all teenagers whose emotions are not understood by the world.

Contents

Preface

The red roses is an anthology consisting of poems soulfully written by Raiyaan kausar A.G. Each poem was penned to express what she felt during her teen phase of life. Her poems describe her and her journey in the last two years of her highschool life.

She hopes the readers can see her life through her poems.

Acknowledgements

My first debt is to my mother who has supported me ever since the beginning, then i would like to thank my teacher Ms. Venus who has helped me hone my writing skills and finally to all those who spared their precious time in reading my work.

Prologue

In a bright room, i cry aloud yet no- one can see. It is not serene yet no-one can hear. I am not new in here but no-one's near. This world seems new to me....

1. Thorns as roses

I wish i was blind
To the eyes connected to my mind;
sore that you are,
Thou has seen unprecedented,
happiness is seldom seen.
O! beautiful things,
Where have you been?
Flooded till flown,
cried till dried.
I am lucky yet you are not.
Behind those chocolate pupils lies a past,
You are a silent witness,
rebuked at times yet the honest one.
How unlucky you are!
I suffer at night;
You are along with me,
better you deserve to see,
still flashes of past steal you glee.
Present ain't any exquisite,
After all, you are a pair of eyes in a girl,
who perceives thorns as roses.

2. The arbor-tristis in my yard

3. I am not perfect

• 3 •

Bruises and scars,
Hugs and kisses,
We are tied by a keyless lock.
We were sweet once,
You were my best friend then.
Are we still the same?
Invisible door it is,
Almost closed,
Do you regret that there's a gap,
Through which we are connected,
An undeniable relation,
Our bond has become
Silently commotional.
I am sorry, I am wrong
To be imperfect,
I coud not be the child you deserve.
I always get on your nerves.
If you could go back in time,
Would you not ask for me
in your prayers anymore?
I am sorry,
I am not perfect.

4. I am blind

I am in my late teens with no eyes,
Standing inside a huge hole with answerless whys'
I jump everytime hoping to perceive climbing up one day but in vain;
Like the smiling memories ebbing away,
As i see the colours of ones whom i relieved to be mine.

5. Rain and my lies

I lie to everyone,

i lie under the rain,

i cry under it, and blame on it.

" Don't cry when you are with me, as people would rebuke me" you

said.

"That's why i am crying now, under the rain" i replied

In a fit of rage, words i spill,

words that hurt,words that i can not take back.

You are good to me,

kindest i have ever met, across the world.

I have met many, but none like thou.

With a friend like you,

In the drizzling rain.

I soothe my heart and cover my wounds.

6. Five years

Sudden changes,
Is it always sudden?
five years and beyond,
it takes for a truth to be true, then I accept it.
Everything has been ephemeral,
Three years is the least.
Five years is the truth.
You and I,
Do not let my love embrace you,
Friends or acquaintances,
Do not come close,
until five years.
If not pierced by words and lost memories would be all that's left.
A lot has been left behind,
I am laid down with ebbing memories and remorseful heart.
I hate myself,
I regret everyday,
I have hurt them all,
Thou, do not become a habit
else again I would revive that moments on a cold day
amidst my new folks
with a smile and gleeful words,
I would hide our past ephemeral memories like
the arbor- tristis.

7. She

She is compelled by the shackle called love,
Her dreams do not matter; for her loved ones selfless as she is,
selfish that they are.
Her heart beats with no emotions
she has lost it all
Patience, dreams and love.
She knows only to obey,
when the little heart says: " No, i am sorry we do not belong to each
other."she says...

8. Shades of grey

I am painted with,
shades of grey on every part,
with the darkest being on my heart.
The joyous yellow timts me a little,
Suffes with the grey later,
I try to smile,
It is involuntary, So I can not.
My heart is darkening every day,
From hues of grey to shades of the darkest days.

9. Where is She?

I am drenched,
under the rain of sadness.
I can not control my emotions
Now, I am a corpse
Where is she?
The innocent little girl, that
I was once.
Alas! She is lost,
unable to come back.
It is in the past
who i was and,
It is not me who was amazing,
Indeed, the life is the reason
for who I was, am and will be.
I am controlled by the universe.
Where is she?
The innocent little girl,
I was once.
She is lost
In the magical past era
Unable to come back.

10. I am growing up

I have changed
I am growing up
My path is completely filled with stones,
I am pierced all over my body,
But
I hope that the blossoms of the spring
can take this bleak of the october away from my life,
I hope time would heal me fill me with
sweetness of life again...

11. That girl

She is going to be there,
She is the one,
The girl who lives across the valley;
She wears her flower printed dress and heads out everyday,
To strive in this ruthless world
It is her,
who can stand up for the right fearlessly,
yet cries over a needle prick.
She has a softer heart,
yet being a strong girl,
She needs to be loved.
I look at her from afar,
She shines bright under the first ray.
Yes,
She is that girl,
I want to be one day.

12. I am fake

From faking a smile,
To all the words I speak,
It is all fake.
The people who trust me,
I break it all knowingly,
I am fake.
With layers of lies,
To makeup my look,
I get ready,
To fake the world.
but,
I remove my masks,
Under the moonlight, every night
Hoping that the moon;
would take away this curse of faking,
In which i am entangled.

13. The poems that are read

• 13 •

Not all poems are written to be read,
Not all words are meant to be heard,
Some are just left hidden
and,
Some are just forgotten, by the poets.
The young depressed me is still alive somewheregiving rise to riots.
I run away from my past,
and the poems describing my lasts.
Not all poems are meant to be read;
and,
Not all memories are remembered.

14. Little did i know

Little did i know,

that my words would be childish.

Every phase, all I hoped was it to remain forever.

"We are forever" I said once.

Little did I know,

It would not last even a day.

All the smiles,

All the fights.

We were so close,

seems not the next day,

I could not keep my words.

Can i rebuke time for that now?

Little did I know,

Nothing would be the same anymore.

Neither my fate nor my words.

Truth it is,

life and the universe are parallel.

Little did I know,

Everything would not want me,

Neither thou nor the fate.

hurt and fallen,

scarred and scared.

Unknown ends,

Would I still smile,

If I think about it in the future?

15. Winds

Those flawless winds,
gandering me,
through my window blinds,
calling me for a secret meet,
As I went obscurely,
They messed my hair,
replenishing their love,
I perceived their presence,
The whizzing air,
The only paraphernalia to call me there,
murmured the magical words,
that pulled my nerval cords,
" You are nature's beauty"
It told me,very boldly,
"You speak" I asked
" I do, cause you're the only girl whom I keek "
A" Why?"
with a helter-skelter
"Cause you're pure as the skies,
and truth is where your heart lies"
Fuddled thoughts rumbling in my mind,
when serenity locked my lips,
The wind passed away,
and I was left gazing......

16. Love of Autumn

Wrapped around my neck;
Orange scarf, eight years old,
golden leaves and golden ground,
The essence of my childhood memories.
When the ten year old me giggled,
As I trip again,
I hear the little girl
laughing and playing with herself,
in her old orange scarf
I hear her giggle and giggle and giggle....

17. The last Christmas

With my oversized jacket,
and striped scarf wrapped on my neck,
I went out dancing to make my snowman ,
On the Christmas Eve,
I inserted my imaginations on the snow
embellishing my front yard,
As I slip and fall into the snow,
Pulling my face out,
I see a man in a red suit,
screaming "Santa is here",
He handed my gifts wishing me,
"Merry Christmas ".

18. The Rain

As I get drenched in the rain,

The petrichor wakes up my memories,

Then as I let the droplets suffuse into my skin,

My memories about you fade away,

My tears flow along the rain, nobody could notice it.

As I swirl and dance with a pirouette;

I perceive the beauty of solitude,

when being watched by mother nature.

Then, when the clouds cry heavily;

I jump higher to feel myself better than ever,

Perhaps, it is true that

Someone's smile lies in someone's tears.

19. She, the poet

When the heart pelts,
when her hands start penning it,
Everything turns into poetry,
and her beautiful soul turns into a poet...

20. Farewell

Our adolescence comes to an end,
We look forward to beautiful inceptions,
And memorable endings.
There is an adrenaline rush,
An urge to be an adult,
Aware of the reality,
Yet excited for it.
It is the unaccepted innocence by the heart,
we all have been reckless,
we are at the end of our teenhood.
With a big smile we all bid farewell,
Unbeknownst to ourselves about what has come to an end.
It is the untold innocence,
That exists in that smile bidding farewell.
That airy- fairy childhood wish has come true.
Now we enter the world,
Yet there is an tinge of solitude exists.
A bundle of fears too.
With a candle of hope,
We all accept it here,
And wave at the memories during this beautiful time,
A part of the journey...

Conclusion

I breathe, wait, hope
    for you to come back,
    To fill my life with colours,
    You took my peace and happiness with you,
    and left me as a live corpse.